GEORGE WASHINGTON CARVER

MORE THAN "THE PEANUT MAN"

By Janel Rodríguez

Illustrated by Subi Bosa

Children's Press®
An imprint of Scholastic Inc.

T0008997

Special thanks to our consultant Gary R. Kremer, executive director, secretary, and librarian of the State Historical Society of Missouri, for his insight into the life and work of George Washington Carver.

Special thanks also to our consultant Dr. Le'Trice Donaldson, assistant professor of history at Texas A&M University-Corpus Christi, for making sure the text of this book is authentic and historically accurate.

Library of Congress Cataloging-in-Publication Data
Names: Rodríguez, Janel, author. | Bosa, Subi, illustrator.
Title: George Washington Carver: More than "the peanut man" / by Janel Rodríguez; illustrated by Subi Bosa.
Description: First edition. | New York, NY : Children's Press, an imprint of Scholastic Inc., 2023. | Series: Bright minds | Includes bibliographical references and index. | Audience: Ages 8–10. | Audience: Grades 4–6. | Summary: "A biography series highlighting the work and social impact of BIPOC inventors"—Provided by publisher.
Identifiers: LCCN 2022028719 (print) | LCCN 2022028720 (ebook) | ISBN 9781338864205 (library binding) | ISBN 9781338864212 (paperback) | ISBN 9781338864229 (ebk)
Subjects: LCSH: Carver, George Washington, 1864?–1943—Juvenile literature. | African American agriculturists—United States—Biography—Juvenile literature. | Agriculturists—United States—Biography—Juvenile literature. | Peanuts—United States—History—Juvenile literature. | BISAC: JUVENILE NONFICTION / Biography & Autobiography / General | JUVENILE NONFICTION / Technology / Inventions | LCGFT: Biographies.
Classification: LCC S417.C3 R53 2023 (print) | LCC S417.C3 (ebook) | DDC 630.92 [B]—dc23/eng/20220711
LC record available at https://lccn.loc.gov/2022028719
LC ebook record available at https://lccn.loc.gov/2022028720

10 9 8 7 6 5 4 3 2 1   23 24 25 26 27

Printed in China   62
First edition, 2023

Book design by Kathleen Petelinsek
Book prototype design by Maria Bergós / Book&Look

Photos ©: 5 center: Historic Collection/Alamy Images; 6 top: Image from the Collections of The Henry Ford; 6 map: Elisa Lara/Dreamstime; 7 top right: Science Source; 9 bottom center: Tuskegee University Archives, Tuskegee University; 10 top right: Jim West/Alamy Images; 11 top right, 11 bottom left: National Park Service; 13 center: Alex Kirkpatrick/The Simpsonian; 15 right: Tuskegee University Archives, Tuskegee University; 16 bottom: Gado/Getty Images; 17 top center: Glasshouse Images/Shutterstock; 18 center: Tuskegee University Archives, Tuskegee University; 19 top right: USDA; 20 top right: Foxyliam/Dreamstime; 22 top right: United States Patent and Trademark Office; 22 bottom left: Tuskegee University Archives, Tuskegee University; 23 top right, 23 center: Tuskegee University Archives, Tuskegee University; 25 center: Chronicle/Alamy Images; 26 center: AP Images; 27 bottom left: Bettmann/Getty Images; 28 top right: Spooner & Wells/Apic/Getty Images; 29 bottom right: Bettmann/Getty Images; 30 top: Dinodia Photos/Getty Images; 32 top left: The Granger Collection; 33 center left: Morphy, Makofsky, Inc.; 33 center right: Fotosearch RM/age fotostock; 40: Author Self Portrait by Janel Rodriguez.

All other photos © Designed by Freepik and Shutterstock.

TABLE OF CONTENTS

★★★★

George Washington Carver *loved* plants!

When he was a young child, he studied plants, painted plants, and looked after them.

He was so good at caring for them that grown-ups gave him a special name: the "Plant Doctor"!

... GEORGE WASHINGTON CARVER

George not only helped plants, he helped people—lots of them—with plants. In fact, his many inventive ideas about how to use plants improved the lives of hundreds of farmers.

I'm sprouting with ideas!

Let's learn more about the life and **legacy** of George Washington Carver!

IN A NUTSHELL

George Washington Carver was likely born in 1864 near **Diamond Grove, Missouri** (he never knew his exact date of birth).

When George was about thirty years old, he settled in Tuskegee, Alabama, and remained there for almost fifty years.

He died on January 5, 1943, at the **Tuskegee Institute**.

George was born in a log cabin. This is what it looked like.

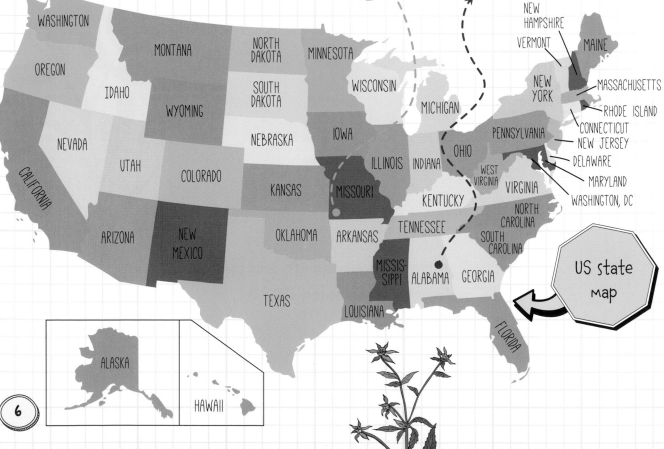

US state map

KNOWN FOR...

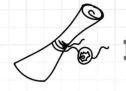

- ☑ Being the "Plant Doctor"

- ☑ His artistic talents

- ☑ His love of **botany** and nature

- ☑ Being the first Black person to earn a graduate degree in **agriculture**

- ☑ Being a tireless scientist

- ☑ Always educating others

- ☑ Endlessly inventing

- ☑ Making the countless qualities of the peanut known

- ☑ Being a man of faith

> Education is the key to unlock the golden door of freedom.

George thought that both sides of education—learning and teaching—were very important. Thanks to going to college he escaped poverty and become a respected scientist. As a teacher, he helped others to build better lives for themselves, too. Education meant freedom.

KIDNAPPED!

George's parents were **enslaved** and worked on farms in Missouri. George and his three siblings were considered enslaved, too. His mother's name was Mary. His father died sometime around when he was born. Soon after, the **Civil War** ended.

WHAT WAS THE CIVIL WAR?
The Civil War started in the United States in 1861. In it, Northern states (called the Union) and Southern states (called the Confederacy) fought against each other over **slavery**. The Union wanted to **abolish** it. The Confederacy wanted to keep it—and even expand it. But the Union won the war in 1865. Later that same year, the Thirteenth Amendment officially abolished slavery in the United States.

Sadly, when George was still a baby, he and his mother were kidnapped by **raiders** who wanted to sell them illegally.

SLAVERY IN AMERICA
For nearly 250 years leading up to the Civil War, Black people had been enslaved in America. They were bought and sold and treated as property. They were taken to plantations all around the South of the United States. There, for many generations, they were forced to work without pay, and many were whipped by their cruel owners. They had no rights as **citizens** or even human beings. It was a terrible way to live.

A NEW FAMILY

The owners of the farm, Moses and Susan Carver, were very upset by this. They hired a neighbor to search for the mother and child. He only found George, and brought him home. George never saw his mother again.

George was a weak baby. A doctor said he would not live past age twenty-one! But, determined to nurse him back to health, the Carvers kept him in their home. As he grew up, Susan taught him how to cook, sew, launder, and garden.

Moses Carver lived to be ninety-eight years old!

SECRET GARDEN

When George was still a boy, he planted a secret garden. It was hidden in a patch of earth not far from the house. He spent his days in the woods, looking for "beauties" (what he called flowers) to gently **uproot** and replant in his garden patch.

This statue depicts a young George as he might have looked when he spent hours in the woods alone.

People in the neighborhood first thought of him as a silly child who wasted his time with flowers. But they soon saw how plants **flourished** under his care. They began going to him for help and advice.

Thank you, Plant Doctor! You're my hero!

That's your "Plant Doctor"? But he's just a kid!

When George was around eleven, the Carvers decided it was time for him to get a formal education. Sadly, in Missouri, it was against the law for Black children to attend school with white children. George left home for an all-Black school. It was eight miles away, in Neosho.

There he lived with a Black couple, Andrew and **Mariah Watkins**.

This is a photo of George taken around the time he was preparing to go off to school.

Mariah, a **midwife** and nurse, taught George how to make medicines out of plants and herbs.

ON HIS OWN

When George was about fourteen, he decided to move to Kansas in search of a better education. But this meant living on his own. To support himself, George got a job cooking for a wealthy white family.

When the Carvers found out, they grew frightened. Traveling alone was really dangerous for a Black child. Also, they thought the hard work would be too much for him. They wanted him to come back home. But George chose to stay.

COLLEGE BOUND

Working to pay for his own clothes and rent (like a grown-up) made going to school difficult. George could only attend classes when he had time. Because of this, he did not complete his high school education until he was in his twenties.

Next, George applied to Highland College in Kansas—and got in! But when they found out he was Black, they rejected him. Some friends recommended he instead try Simpson College, a school in Iowa. He did and was accepted.

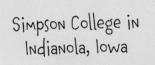

Simpson College in Indianola, Iowa

HANGING ON A STRING

To pay for school, George started a laundry service. At first, he barely had any customers—and so he barely had any money for food. But when fellow students heard about his situation, they spread the word that he needed help. Then the students, teachers, and townspeople all became his customers.

George enjoyed his time at Simpson. He was treated like an equal to any other student there. He found that everyone around him seemed to genuinely want to help him. He felt seen as a human being.

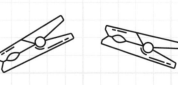

ALWAYS THE ARTIST

In school, George studied art and piano. He had dreams of becoming an artist and a teacher. But his art teacher, Etta Budd, persuaded him to **transfer** to Iowa State University's College of Agriculture. There, he would be able to study botany. He did and was an excellent student.

But George never stopped painting. In fact, in 1893, he entered a **painting** he'd made of yucca and cactus plants into a contest at the World's Fair in Chicago. He won an honorable mention!

George painted what he loved most of all, of course: artworks of plants and flowers! They are called "botanicals."

Many years later, George had his photograph taken next to that painting.

THE ORIGIN OF THE "W"
While in school, George discovered there was another student also named "George Carver." People kept confusing them with each other! To fix this, George added a "W" (and later "Washington") to his name.

PROFESSOR CARVER

When George graduated in 1894, the school invited him to stay and join their staff to continue working in the lab studying plant disease. He was happy to accept, and in two years, he also earned another degree: a master's in agriculture.

That same year, 1896, a man named **Booker T. Washington** approached George and asked him to join the Tuskegee Institute in Alabama. George accepted the invitation!

I just love being in my favorite place doing my favorite thing day after day!

WHO WAS BOOKER T. WASHINGTON?

Booker T. Washington was a prominent Black American leader, speaker, writer, and educator. He was also an advisor to presidents! He is best known for heading the Tuskegee Institute (now University). It was formed to teach Black Americans how to make a living and support themselves.

Professor Carver sits with the staff of the Tuskegee Institute's Agricultural Department in 1902.

This is going to be harder than I thought.

But I have an idea...

MR. CARVER

At first, George's students in Alabama did not want to learn agriculture. Most of their parents had worked with crops as enslaved persons, and they wanted to get out of farm life. They wanted to learn something new! Besides, what could George teach them that they didn't already know?

But eventually they would learn that George had much to teach them— and their parents.

REACHING OUT...

George figured out that a way to reach out to the poorest farmers in the area was to bring school to them! Every month, he would go to the fields, visit the farmers where they were working, and teach them right there. Some of the farmers were his students' parents.

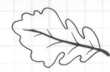

George made his farm trips in a **"Jesup"** wagon—a horse-pulled "school on wheels"—which he designed himself.

It was named after Morris Jesup, the New York banker who **funded** the program.

QUOTE:
"It has always been the one great ideal of my life to be of the greatest good to the greatest number of 'my people' [as] possible."

George filled it with tools and supplies that he would give to the farmers free of charge.

He met with many, many farmers this way!

18

AND TEACHING

He also produced a series of booklets that he distributed to the farmers.

A sample of one of the booklets, which he called **"bulletins"**

Between 1898 and 1943, George wrote and distributed forty-four of them!

They offered useful advice on different topics, such as caring for soil, eating right, and preserving food. They also included smart and healthy money-saving tips. One of them was to feed pigs acorns instead of store-bought feed.

oink!

Don't be such a hog!

TURNING POINT

One of the best ways George helped farmers escape poverty was by teaching them about crop rotation.

For years they had planted only one crop: cotton. This had tired out the soil and made it lose its nutrients. Unable to grow cotton, the farmers found themselves without a crop, without money, and without hope.

George taught the farmers that, if they took turns raising different crops on their land, like peanuts, soybeans, and sweet potatoes, it would both give the soil a rest and enrich it, too.

> When the crops take turns, they enrich the soil and help the other crops grow.

PEANUT

SOYBEAN

SWEET POTATO

SEASON 1   SEASON 2   SEASON 3

BUMPER CROPS

Farmers who tried crop rotation had great success. They suddenly found themselves with more peanuts, soybeans, and sweet potatoes than they knew what to do with.

George then made it his business to find new uses for the crops. He found ways to turn them into other food products like vinegars, **molasses**, and flour. He also created many household products from them, such as laundry soap, shaving cream, oils, glue, printing ink, and **antiseptics**.

It's nuts how many sweet potatoes I have!

It's sweet how many peanuts I have!

PRUNE AND PEANUT ICE CREAM
(as written by George Washington Carver)

Ingredients:
2 cups of milk

3 egg yolks

½ pound of pulp from well-cooked and sweetened prunes

1 quart of heavy cream

½ cup of blanched and ground peanuts

1 teaspoon vanilla extract

Preparation: Heat the milk, then pour it into the well-beaten egg yolk. Blend all the other ingredients thoroughly. Freeze and serve in dainty glasses.

George invented hundreds and hundreds of products! But he only patented inventions for three of them. His first **patent** (received on January 6, 1925) was for a pomade (or cream) made from peanuts. It was used to take care of the hair and the scalp.

WHAT IS A PATENT?
A patent is a legal document. It gives an inventor the right to be the only person to make and sell what they invented.

This patent for the pomade gives detailed instructions on how to make it.

Patented Jan. 6, 1925.   1,522,176

UNITED STATES PATENT OFFICE.

GEORGE WASHINGTON CARVER, OF TUSKEGEE, ALABAMA.

COSMETIC AND PROCESS OF PRODUCING THE SAME.

No Drawing.   Application filed September 17, 1923. Serial No. 663,302.

To all whom it may concern:

Be it known that I, GEORGE WASHINGTON CARVER, a citizen of the United States, residing at Tuskegee, in the county of Macon and State of Alabama, have invented new ...ed or usual tint, ...having powder combined ...carry out the process, the peanuts ...utilized in their raw, boiled or blanched ...dition and are first ground or macerated ...any desired manner to the fineness of peanut butter. If for any reason a granular pomade is desired the grinding of the peanuts is carried out only to the extent necessary to give the character desired to the finished product. When ground to the fineness of peanut butter as suggested the resulting product will be a perfectly smooth substance.

To the ground or macerated nuts taking as a basis one ounce of peanuts there is next added 100 c. c. of pure water either hot or cold which is well stirred in with the ground nuts.

The resulting mixture is then strained through a piece of cheese cloth with gentle pressure and is put on the stove or ...th and evaporated until the oil ...visible on the surface. ...ulting product ...

...modified ...peanut oil may be added and the entire mass stirred until it becomes of the consistency of thick cream.

The material is then removed from the fire and approximately six grams of toilet powder such as kaolin, kaolinite, or china clay (preferably having slight fuller's earth properties) is added and the combined mass is thoroughly mixed until it becomes a thick heavy cream.

A quantity of salicylic acid substantially the size of a small pea, 10 drops of benzoin, and three or four drops of any desired perfume are then added. The mass thus ob-...tained is finally ground or macerated until absolutely smooth, if the smooth product is desired, and the product is packed in porcelain, or glass containers.

If desired the above process may be modified by omitting either the added peanut oil, or the toilet powders, or both. By proper choice of the toilet powder any desired color may be given the product, from the dark ...shades through the pinks, lavender... ...ure white.

...rocess of producing a cosmetic ...ises reducing peanuts to a finely ...tion, diluting the product with ...g the mass to a consistency of ...and adding a preservative

...s of producing a cosmetic ...reducing peanuts to a finely ...n, adding peanut oil and a ...reto and reducing the mass ...of thick cream.

...s of producing a cosmetic ...reducing peanuts to a finely ...n, diluting the product, add-...r and a preservative there-...g the mass to a consistency of ...

...ocess of producing a cosmetic ...ises reducing peanuts to a finely ...ndition, diluting with water, heat-...mixture, adding peanut oil and a ...ative and reducing the mass to a con-...cy of thick cream.

...The process of producing cosmetics ...which comprises reducing peanuts to a finely divided condition, diluting the product, evaporating until oil appears upon the surface, adding peanut oil, toilet powder and a preservative.

6. The process of producing cosmetics which comprises reducing peanuts to a finely divided condition, diluting the product, straining the diluted mass, evaporating until oil appears upon the surface, adding peanut oil, stirring toilet powder into the mass, adding a preservative and a perfume and macerating until smooth.

7. The process of producing a cosmetic which comprises reducing peanuts to a finely divided condition, diluting with water, straining, evaporating until oil appears upon the surface, adding peanut oil, stirring

George even created a small line of **cosmetics** from peanut oil. He used the money he made to fund his work helping others.

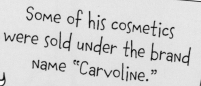

Some of his cosmetics were sold under the brand name "Carvoline."

The second and third patents (received on June 9, 1925, and June 14, 1927) were for wall paints and stains. The stains were for darkening or lightening the appearance of wood furnishings and floors.

George offered many colors and shades. He was inspired by the colors he found in nature. George sold them at low prices to give poor farmers an easy way to make their homes beautiful. They were also used on the walls at Tuskegee Institute!

These are samples of some of the paint colors he offered. Some of them were made from clay.

If you look closely, you can see a miniature nature scene that George painted with the colors he created.

THE PEANUT MAN

Peanuts were George's favorite crop of all. He often praised their properties.

Peanut crops can be grown in the same years you grow cotton, since they grow at different times of the season.

They produce their own nitrogen, which enriches the soil they are in.

They are high in calories, full of protein, and very nutritious.

PEANUT RECIPE IDEAS
(by George Washington Carver)

Peanut soup
Peanut sauce
Peanut bread
Peanut cookies
Peanut muffins
Peanut doughnuts
Peanut bars
Peanut rolls
Peanut cakes
Peanut pudding
Peanut patties
Peanut omelets
Peanut macaroni
Peanut salad
"Mock meat"

VISITING THE CAPITOL

In 1921, the Peanut Association of America asked George to speak on their behalf before members of **Congress** in the US Capitol. They wanted to have a tariff (tax) on **imported** peanuts approved. But first they needed George to prove how important the peanut crop was to America.

WHAT IS CONGRESS?
Congress is the part of government that makes the nation's laws. It is made up of two parts: the Senate and the House of Representatives. The members of Congress meet in the United States Capitol in Washington, DC.

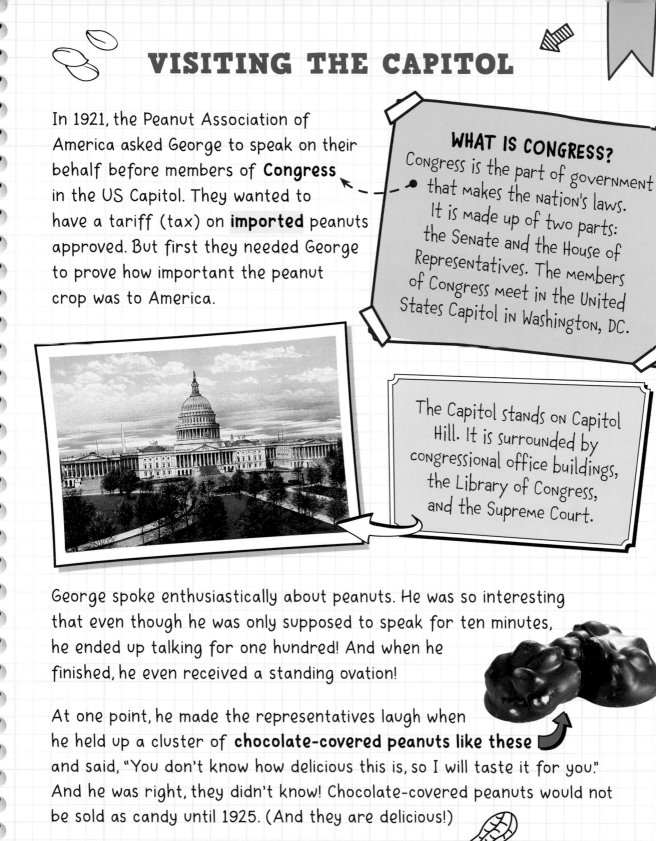

The Capitol stands on Capitol Hill. It is surrounded by congressional office buildings, the Library of Congress, and the Supreme Court.

George spoke enthusiastically about peanuts. He was so interesting that even though he was only supposed to speak for ten minutes, he ended up talking for one hundred! And when he finished, he even received a standing ovation!

At one point, he made the representatives laugh when he held up a cluster of **chocolate-covered peanuts like these** and said, "You don't know how delicious this is, so I will taste it for you." And he was right, they didn't know! Chocolate-covered peanuts would not be sold as candy until 1925. (And they are delicious!)

FAME...AND RACISM

After his speech before Congress, George became known as the "Peanut Man." Articles about his genius were published in magazines and newspapers. They made him **internationally** famous. He met important people. But even as he was admired around the world, he still had to deal with **racism**.

George Washington Carver and President Franklin D. Roosevelt

George was a peaceful man. He avoided conflict. Although **segregation** laws were unjust, he followed them—even if this meant entering through the back doors of lecture halls for events where he was the main speaker!

JIM CROW LAWS
At that time, "Jim Crow" laws existed in many parts of the United States, especially in the South. They separated Black people from white people in public spaces. This was called "segregation." The laws made it illegal for Black people to sit in restaurants, in the front seats of buses, or even to enter buildings through front doors.

He did not join protests or marches, but he desired peace between different races of people. Between 1923 and 1933, he traveled the United States promoting equal rights for Black people. He drew large crowds—even at white Southern colleges—and spoke in his distinctive high-pitched voice and good-humored, gentlemanly manner.

keep your thoughts free from hate, and you need have no fear from those who hate you!

Segregation in public education was declared illegal in 1954 with the landmark *Brown v. Board of Education* decision. This was eleven years after George passed away.

In the 1930s, George and Henry Ford began writing letters to each other.

WHO WAS HENRY FORD?

Henry Ford was an American businessman. He was famous for his design of the Model T Ford car and for **revolutionizing** the way cars were made in factories. His idea to use **conveyor belts** on assembly lines allowed cars to be "mass-produced"—that is, quickly and cheaply made. This also helped to make cars more affordable to the average American.

Henry Ford sitting in his first car design, the "Quadricycle." Yes, those are bicycle wheels!

They each greatly admired the other's work and in time would become close friends.

Let's be BFFs!

I'm your biggest fan.

GREAT CHEMISTRY

George and Henry Ford both had a strong interest in "chemurgy." This is a term used to describe the turning of raw farm products into useful things (other than something to eat), such as paper, paint, fiber, plastic, or fuel.

The two men would meet and share ideas. Together, they worked on ways of making plastics out of soybeans. They also invented a rubber substitute from **goldenrod**.

They were also both interested in healthy eating. They developed a sandwich spread made of a number of plants, such as purslane, pigweed, milkweed, dandelion, and wild radish.

George and Henry Ford enjoyed a friendship that lasted for many years.

HELPING A GREAT SOUL

George became famous for his knowledge of agriculture. This caught the attention of the Indian political activist **Mahatma Gandhi**.

WHO WAS MAHATMA GANDHI?
Mahatma Gandhi led India to successfully win its **independence** from Great Britain. He accomplished this not by war, but through the effective use of peaceful protests.

He was called Mahatma. It means "Great Soul."

Gandhi read about George's work with the farmers in Alabama. He wondered if George could help Indian farmers with some advice.

George admired Gandhi and was eager to help. George sent him bulletins filled with farming tips. George knew Gandhi was a vegetarian. In letters calling him "dear friend," George advised Gandhi to eat products made with whole wheat flour, corn, peanuts, soy, and fruits native to India to build up his strength.

Flour

U.S.

India

IN THE SPIRIT

George was a **devout Christian**. His favorite way to pray was to talk to God while taking early morning nature walks. It was during these times that he got the ideas that led to his discoveries.

> Nothing is more beautiful than the loveliness of the woods before sunrise.

BARTRAM TRAIL

That's why he never patented most of his products. He believed they were God's ideas—not his. Plus, there were hundreds of them—too many to patent. Finally, George wanted his discoveries to benefit as many people as possible.

HIS LAST YEARS

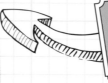

When he grew old, George became frail and sickly—like he had been as a baby. Seeing this, Henry Ford kindly arranged to have an elevator installed in his friend's home. This eased George's daily trips to the laboratory, on the floor below, and back to his room upstairs.

This is George working in his lab around 1940.

George died on January 5, 1943, at the age of 78. He was buried on Tuskegee's campus, next to Booker T. Washington's grave.

His life savings of $60,000 were used to found the George Washington Carver Institute for Agriculture at Tuskegee. Even in death, he was still able to help others.

This sentence is engraved on George's **tombstone**. It shows he lived a modest life.

GEORGE WASHINGTON CARVER

He could have added fortune to fame, but caring for neither, he found happiness and honor in being helpful to the world.

LEGACY

Education was VERY important to George. So it makes sense that there are a number of schools now named after him. This includes an elementary school in Newark, New Jersey, a middle school in Los Angeles, California, and a high school in New Orleans, Louisiana.

George Washington Carver High School in New Orleans, Louisiana

There are also the George Washington Carver museums located in Missouri, Alabama, and Texas. But perhaps most impressive of all is the national **monument** that was built in his honor in Diamond, Missouri. It was the first-ever made for an American who was not a president of the United States.

The monument includes a large bust of George. It stands in the farm where he was born and spent his childhood.

And now one word of advice from the mind of George Washington Carver:

QUOTE:
"Young people...always keep your eyes open to what Mother Nature has to teach you. By so doing you will learn many valuable things every day of your life."

During his lifetime and afterward, George came to be much more than the "Peanut Man."

YOUR TURN!

George Washington Carver lived by these eight rules that he liked to share with his students:

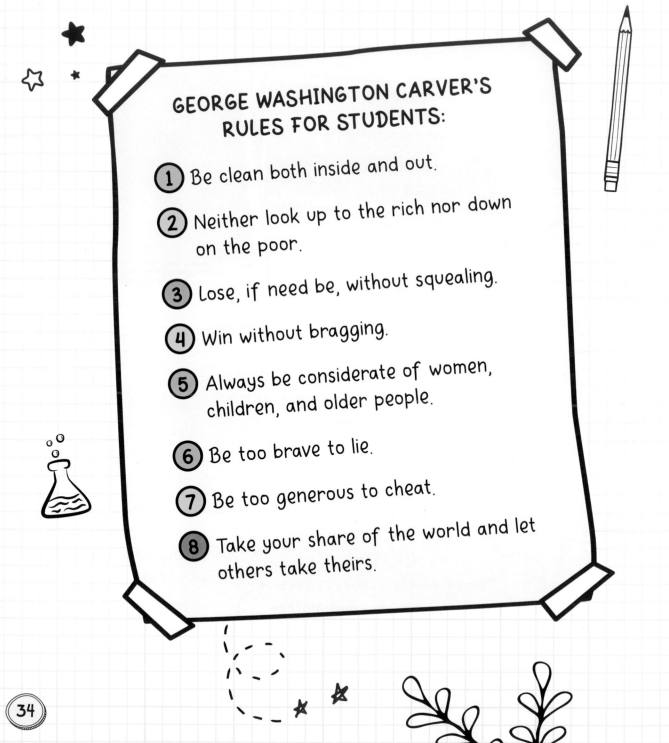

GEORGE WASHINGTON CARVER'S RULES FOR STUDENTS:

1. Be clean both inside and out.
2. Neither look up to the rich nor down on the poor.
3. Lose, if need be, without squealing.
4. Win without bragging.
5. Always be considerate of women, children, and older people.
6. Be too brave to lie.
7. Be too generous to cheat.
8. Take your share of the world and let others take theirs.

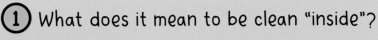

READ THE RULES CAREFULLY.

NOW ANSWER THESE QUESTIONS:

1. What does it mean to be clean "inside"?

2. What did George mean when he said not to "squeal" when you lose?

3. Which rule do you think is the most important? Why?

4. Which rule is the easiest to follow? Which rule is the hardest?

5. What are ways you can be considerate of older people?

6. Why is it brave to tell the truth?

7. Do you think it is possible to live your life following these eight rules?

GLOSSARY

abolish (uh-BAH-lish) to put an end to something officially

agriculture (AG-ri-kuhl-chur) the raising of crops and animals; farming

antiseptics (an-ti-SEP-tiks) substances that kill germs and prevent infection by stopping the growth of germs

botany (BAH-tuh-nee) the scientific study of plant life

bulletins (BUL-i-tinz) official statements or brief news summaries

Christian (KRIS-chuhn) a person who follows the religion based on the life and teachings of Jesus

citizens (SIT-i-zuhnz) people who have the full rights and protection of a particular country, such as a right to live there, to work there, and to vote in the country's elections

conveyor belts (kuhn-VAY-ur belts) continuous moving bands of fabric, rubber, or metal used for moving objects from one place to another

cosmetics (kahz-MET-iks) beauty products; makeup

devout (di-VOUT) deeply religious

enslaved (en-SLAYVD) unfair condition of being owned by another person

flourished (FLUR-isht) to have grown well

funded (FUHN-duhd) to have provided money for a special purpose

goldenrod (GOHL-duhn-rahd) a tall, wild plant with short spikes of small, yellow flowers

imported (im-POR-tuhd) to have brought into a place or country from somewhere else

independence (in-di-PEN-duhns) freedom; the condition of being independent

internationally (in-tur-NASH-uh-nuh-lee) involving more than one country

legacy (LEG-uh-see) something handed down from one generation to another

midwife (MID-wife) a person who is trained to help women give birth

molasses (muh-LAS-iz) a thick, dark, sweet syrup made when sugarcane is processed into sugar

monument (MAHN-yuh-muhnt) a statue, building, or other structure that reminds people of an event or a person

nitrogen (NYE-truh-juhn) a colorless, odorless gas that makes up about four-fifths of the earth's atmosphere

patent (PAT-uhnt) a legal document giving the inventor of an item the sole rights to manufacture or sell it for a certain period of time

racism (RAY-si-zuhm) the belief that a particular race is better than others; treating people unfairly or cruelly because of their race

raiders (RAY-durz) people who stage sudden, surprise attacks on places or people

revolutionizing (rev-uh-LOO-shuh-nye-zing) bringing about a complete change in something

segregation (seg-ri-GAY-shuhn) the act or practice of keeping people or groups apart, as in racial segregation

slavery (SLAY-vur-ee) unfair condition in which one human being is owned by another

tombstone (TOOM-stone) a carved block of stone that marks the place where someone is buried

transfer (TRANS-fur) to change from one school to another

uproot (uhp-ROOT) to tear or pull out by the roots

INDEX

FURTHER READING

Aliki. *A Weed Is a Flower: The Life of George Washington Carver.* New York: Aladdin, 1988.

Barretta, Gene, and Frank Morrison. *The Secret Garden of George Washington Carver.* New York: Katherine Tegen Books, 2020.

Driscoll, Laura. *George Washington Carver: The Peanut Wizard.* New York: Grosset & Dunlap, 2003.

Gigliotti, Jim. *Who Was George Washington Carver?* New York: Penguin Workshop, 2015.

Read the other books in this series:

ABOUT THE AUTHOR

Janel Rodríguez is a "Nuyorican"—that is, a Puerto Rican who was born and raised in New York City. She wrote the book *Super SHEroes of History: Civil Rights* for Scholastic. Like George Washington Carver, she is an artist. But unlike him, she is not good at looking after plants— but she wishes she was!

ABOUT THE ILLUSTRATOR

As a child, Subi Bosa drew pictures all the time, in every room of the house—sometimes even on the walls! His mother always told everyone, "He knew how to draw before he could properly hold a pencil." Today, Subi continues to draw fun picture books, comics, and graphic novels from his home in Cape Town, a city in South Africa. He has won many awards for his work!